Personal Astronomy

poems by

Sally Zakariya

Finishing Line Press
Georgetown, Kentucky

Personal Astronomy

Copyright © 2018 by Sally Zakariya
ISBN 978-1-63534-641-1 First Edition
All rights reserved under International and Pan-American Copyright Conventions. No part of this book may be reproduced in any manner whatsoever without written permission from the publisher, except in the case of brief quotations embodied in critical articles and reviews.

ACKNOWLEDGMENTS

I am grateful to the following publications, in which these poems appeared, sometimes in slightly different forms.

Bacopa Literary Review, Theory of Omission, 2017
Connecticut River Review: Lunar Eclipse, 2015
Edge: Since Last Wednesday, Volume 8, 2014
Emerge Literary Journal: Funeral, Winter 2013
Existere, Constellations, Issue 37.1, Fall/Winter 2017/2018
Gyroscope Review: Stargazing, Summer 2017
Kaaterskill Basin Literary Journal: Life on Mars, Winter 2017
Magnolia Review: Meditation on a French Fry, Issue 4, 2016
Rat's Ass Review: What I Would Tell the Fortune Teller, January 2016; After the Eclipse, Winter 2017
The Northern Virginia Review: Mackerel Sky, Spring 2015
Theodate: Mother Whistling in Heaven, Summer 2013
When You Escape (chapbook published by Five Oaks Press): May Meteor Shower and Between the Words, 2016

Publisher: Leah Maines
Editor: Christen Kincaid
Cover Art: Detail from a star chart by Johann Elert Bode (1747-1826)
Author Photo: Mohamed Zakariya
Cover Design: Elizabeth Maines McCleavy

Printed in the USA on acid-free paper.
Order online: www.finishinglinepress.com
      also available on amazon.com

      Author inquiries and mail orders:
           Finishing Line Press
           P. O. Box 1626
      Georgetown, Kentucky 40324
           U. S. A.

Contents

May Meteor Shower 1
Constellations 2
Stargazing 3
November Sky 4
Afternoon Sun 5
The Look of Evening 6
Lunar Eclipse 7
Mother Whistling in Heaven 8
Funeral 9
Dispatches from Beyond 10
Since Last Wednesday 11
Theory of Omission 12
Full Moon 13
Dark Matter 14
Mackerel Sky 15
Hole in the Sky 16
After the Eclipse 17
Knot in the Universe 18
What I Would Tell the Fortune Teller 19
Meditation on a French Fry 20
Between the Words 21
Much to Tell 22
Life on Mars 23
Thank You Note to the Universe 24

*For Zak, the fixed star
in my universe*

May Meteor Shower

The surprising thing is being here
with you—you of all the sky's bright stars
you of all the planets and the comets
a blip of coincidence in a random universe
a confluence of two collections of atoms
tumbling together in supernova
or something like it.

Forgive my astronomical hyperbole
my celestial excess, but tonight
the constellation Camelopardalis
will celebrate us with a rain of meteors
streaking across the sky (or so we're told)
each one blazing and burning
winking for us.

And if we can't see them they will still
be there, stitching the skies together
with needles of light so fast and fine
it would take God's eye to see the seams.

Meanwhile, below, I search the stationary
stars to find the source of light reflected
in your eyes.

Constellations

> *Why did not somebody teach me the constellations,*
> *and make me at home in the starry heavens, which*
> *are always overhead?* —Thomas Carlyle

I know night's huntsman Orion
with his bright belt and sword
and the Dipper pointing North
but the others are just names
scattered among the stars.

And oh so many stars—
I never knew how many
until we left the city lights
and drove up the mountain.

We stood amazed like the old Greeks
dwarfed by the enormity of night.

How did they find order in that cloud
of radiance, that vast crowd of stars?

It's not how but why that matters—
to name what they could not know
to explain the inexplicable
to feel at home in the universe.

Friends showed me Cassiopeia
and the two bears, or tried to,
but I was lost in the light,
looking to fix patterns in my
mind to make my own
comforting constellations.

Stargazing

When stars fall, I want to see
the furious streaks of light
they scribe across the sky.

Camping in California, you said,
you could count the shooting stars,
but here in the East our city lights
hemorrhage into the heavens,
obscuring who knows what
astronomical marvels.

I'd like to think a comet
arced across the continent
the year that we were born,
wonder of wonders—two
polar opposites—the twain
they said would never meet.

I'd like to think a falling star
landed near you on a California
hill, pointing you toward the East
to pluck me from my lonely life
and brighten my star-lost nights.

November Sky

Daytime

Sky changes her clothes
moonstone gray tinged
with palest yellow
blue draped with
translucent drifts
of cloud and then
from her closet
finger-paint streaks
of red and gold
before the dark.

Nighttime

Black is a net of stars
with a circle ripped
open for the moon.
Black is bare branches
fanned across the sky
black on black.
Black is patched
with window light
with someone
looking out.
Black is tonight.
Tomorrow
the sky will be
gray again.

Afternoon Sun

Lazing after lunch I slit my eyes
against the afternoon sun
incandescent through the slatted shade
a gauzy shower
        of iridescent filaments

Yesterday Venus crossed the sun
a small dark disc
against that great light
moving slowly as a mote
transits the universe
        of your eye
side to side then gone

I close my eyes and see
an afterimage of us
as we were in early morning
fresh and full of expectation
dimming now
        as evening nears

The Look of Evening

An intermingling of day and night
past early but far from late
a sense of never-ending twilight

Crystalline daylight tarnished
streetlights haloed in hazy glow
shadows cast in grayscale
colors of day fading to black

Down the street a young couple
embrace in an entranceway
silhouetted against the dim gleam
of a front-door light

Their faces obscured, I conjure
them in imagination—
the 5 o'clock shadow on his chin
the shaded hollow of her cheek
the look of evening in their eyes

Lunar Eclipse

Dear Moon,
          In bed tonight, cat at my feet, I sleep right
through your eclipse, miss what they call your blood
moon, red and full, expectant as Earth's shadow moves
across your eager face

I wake to the sound of rain washing the eaves, bathing
sparrows and titmice as they light on the feeder
singing morning songs, the sodden sky still
dim, its own eclipse

I thought I had plenty of time to track your persistent
path from silver sliver to round radiance
oh luminous companion, keeper of days, puller
of tides, breeder of dreams

but the day is dark and will grow darker so I must
take on faith your stately movement up
from the horizon to trace the sky's wide dome
tonight and every night to come

Mother Whistling in Heaven

Thrifty in everything except your love
for the parade of dogs who walked

at your heel—Dusty, Skipper, Finnegan—
good dogs, they came when you whistled

and so did we until the mockingbird learned
to whistle too, a lesson in bird song and

who you can trust. You taught us how
to know trees and wildflowers and how

to can tomatoes and peaches and store them
on the dim shelves under the basement stairs.

Depression-schooled, you turned sheets
top to bottom and sewed us party dresses

out of parachute silk brought back from
Japan by Uncle Ralph and dyed rose pink.

And if they joined you in your heaven, those
Japanese pilots the silk was meant to save,

they would drift, bowing, into your
billowy pink cloud. No more war now,

no more making do, just smoking cigarettes,
playing bridge, whistling for the dogs.

Funeral

It's a grand send-off the Catholics give you
with their candles and incense and the constant
up and down of the prayers and also the
calm certainty of the priest's homily.

Around me everyone knows the words
and when to kneel and I'm fairly sure
the man in the coffin knew the words
to all the hymns and all the prayers as well.

He was a good man and a good neighbor
says the priest *and Jesus will be waiting
for him on the other side of the bridge.*
I can't conjure up that bridge in my

skeptic's mind but I can see the divine
origami of the ceiling with its manifold
angles within angles, peaks within peaks
and then the geometry of the leaded windows
marking out a straight path upward.

Dispatches from Beyond

London winter ... gray ... implacable
me still bleeding from a broken heart

We come to this chill hall to hear dispatches
from beyond delivered by a ruddy British
housewife all twin set and brogues

*I have a message for someone who has come
across the sea* the spiritualist says
I feel her eyes on me

*a message from an old woman on the other
side—keep something of hers and everything
will be all right* she says

I touch Grandmother's little cross
on its silver chain—maybe it's Granny
come to comfort me in death as she
had never done in life

she who drank sherry every evening
from a crystal glass served on a silver tray
who dressed for dinner in long velvet gowns
who wore a cameo on ribbon at her throat

I shiver, almost wanting to believe
but no—the trifling cross meant nothing
to her and little more to me

no—this imperious woman would have
shunned the man who left me
the man whose skin was black

no—the so-called message is for no one
in particular—just anyone who seeks
to snatch a word of solace from beyond

Since Last Wednesday

The world has gone on
the wheels turned
lives began and ended
birds announced the morning
again and again
as though nothing changed
as though no blind
cleaver had cut last
Wednesday from all
days before or after
and left it standing
alone somewhere
sidelined as the great
spiral took the rest
of us on its relentless way
sightseers in time
and space but without
you along to share
the ride

Theory of Omission

A sparrow rests on the rusted
fencepost, its red-brown feathers
echoing the rust

Omit the sparrow and the thought
of *bird* remains, mental excavation
discovering what is no longer there

So it is with loss

That which is removed, remains
that which never was, hovers
on the edge of existence

You who are now gone
        you who never were
my archaeology creates you—
sparrows that do not rest
on any fencepost

Full Moon

Rising like a bubble in champagne
you break the surface of the sky
up over the horizon's rim
your smooth ascent a stately
transformation from blood orange
to gold to silver as the night
darkens with modesty
to receive you

Dark Matter

Focus on the tip of your nose
says the science guy on the radio
*and while you do, thousands
of particles of dark matter
will bombard it*

Turns out there's no such thing
as empty space—what isn't us
or planets and stars is something
unknown, invisible, impalpable

They call it dark matter, dark energy
it's everywhere, it's most of everything

It's hard to wrap your head around
this stuff, but when you do
you see how right it is

How little we know of each other
of what matters to you, or you, or you
of what energy you spend, what
happiness, what hurts propel you

Life's passage is from dark to dark
from mystery to mystery
learning one another is our first task
while we live here in the light

Mackerel Sky

A clutch of feathers almost
unrecognizable
         as the bird it once was
lies unnoticed by the grocery carts
lined up outside the market

Empty of life, fallen in on itself, but still
the artful design of gray and white and brown
         the delicate stipple

I am the instability of all things, at all levels,
says the bird, in silence

Dappled clouds like fish scales, like speckled
         feathers, swim the sky

Hole in the Sky
    August 21, 2017

Wheels within wheels
the wonder of it
the precision
the exclusivity—
      our blinding blazing sun
          our perfectly placed moon—
a celestial dance performed
for our planet alone

The Sun was put to shame
and went down in the daytime
said a Babylonian sky watcher
and the Sun has perished
out of the heavens wrote Homer

A world in awe marks the days still
predicts the path of the moon's shadow
shields its eyes against the fiery corona

But miles from the totality
I can only dream of darkness a million
      times darker than day
only imagine still silence when birds
      cease their singing
only guess the sudden shivery drop
      in temperature

In honor of the eclipse
I set aside digital clocks
turn instead to an old clockwork
      timepiece—
faint human echo of a universe
      in motion

After the Eclipse

And then it's over—the midday darkness lifts,
the moon loses its fiery crown, the sun returns full force.

The same yet different—something has changed.
A few minutes' suspension of the day's discord

and we are put in our place, mere spectators for once,
relinquishing our audacious sense of agency and control.

A slim thumbnail of light and millions stand amazed,
humbled, no longer masters of the universe.

A two-minute reprieve, a chance for contemplation,
for reflection, before the world turns on its wounded way.

Knot in the Universe

When we walk through that door
we know we won't be turning back.

Two dwindling stars circling a black hole—
the inevitable gravity holds us spellbound,
enthralled, in a dance of captivation.

How close can we come before we reach
the point of no return, succumbing
to the power of that implacable pull?

A knot has been tied in the universe
that cannot be untied.

What I Would Tell the Fortune Teller

I believe in serendipity, the chance
conjunction of an improbable pair
the two you'd never think
would come together or if they did
you'd never think would stick

I believe in the fortune cookie fortune
the message in a bottle that brings
a sea-stained treasure map
the four-leaf clover that delivers
gold and glory

I believe in reading palms and cards
and stars and all the other tricks
soothsayers use to show us
what they say will come and yes
of course the crystal ball

But mostly I believe in chance—
in possibility—I put my faith
in happenstance, the fluke that brought
the two of us together and somehow
made it all come right

Meditation on a French Fry

You're saving the crispy ones
stacking them log-wise
kindling in a fireplace
a fire to light your way
    you tell me

It takes more than that
I think, having lost my way
somewhere between the yes
of wanting and the no
    of hesitation

Angled across the stack
a perfect fry glistens oil and salt
its skin left on to prove provenance
to guarantee an origin in the ground

which is where we begin and end
grubby, humble, having dreamed
our lives away, somnambulists
between first wakening
    and final sleep

Between the Words

Nature has the last word,
always does, so when I send
you a message in a bottle,
the sea scrubs the ink off
the paper, and when the bottle
washes up ashore, the sand
welcomes a long-lost
brother, somehow evolved
into glass without the hell
of the furnace.

And when I sing a song
for you in my old voice,
cracked and off key,
a blustery breeze
blows the tune away,
and finches drown
me out with their own
avian halleluiah
chorus, praising sun
and seeds and airy
acrobatics.

So instead I write you
a poem with imaginary
spaces between each word,
spaces so deep and wide
there's room for both of us,
and as you read, the clock
ticks slowly—so slowly
nature's daily round
will seem to last
forever.

Much to Tell

> *That there is so much to tell now, really now.*
> —John Ashbery, "As We Know," 1979

There is so much to tell Ashbery wrote,
and yes the story's long when you start
before the beginning, where stories
truly start.

Most start in clouds, in sky and stars,
and then some complex story line—
caterpillar into butterfly, or maybe moth,
dusty wings, feathery feelers, seeking
the light.

Picture them tumbling by the thousands,
fluttering at dusk, all unaware their time
will soon be up.

And our time as well, flutter as we may,
shaking off the dust, seeking the light,
telling our constant stories to the birds,
to the rain, to any poor soul who might
be listening.

There is much to tell—about the pen,
the words, the paper we write on,
the work, the slack and sleep, the joy,
and all the rest, about we two, then three,
now two again and getting on, counting
our story's days from *Once upon a time*
until *The end.*

Life on Mars

Perhaps we were always approaching
this alien rock, these ghost seas
strangers together, breathless in the thin air
two orbiters, sometimes in sync
      always out of place

Back then we would dream this journey
the two of us circling like swifts
      soaring on wind
sweet scent of being rising from earth
warm sunlight bathing our backs

And then the stones, the empty seas

We stay aloft, outsiders to everything
      but each other
savoring the unexpected, the extraordinary
      rightness of arriving

Thank You Note to the Universe

> *First-seen neutron star collision creates light, gravitational waves and gold.* —CNN, October 16, 2017

At a far edge of the universe, dense stars
circled in a dance of attraction millions of years ago,
found consummation in a shower of gold.

Listening now here on earth, we catch
their faint cry of collision, see the fireball flash and fade,
feel ripples in the fabric of the cosmos.

Is this where Greek Zeus learned to veil
himself in a rain of golden coins, a ploy to ravish
Danae in her locked room, unaware?

Had he roamed the galaxies to gather
the stars' elemental gifts—silver, platinum, uranium,
gold for the world's wedding rings?

We look to the skies for treasure, take
cosmic gifts for granted and grub away for more
never mind the existential cost to Earth.

How proud we are of our knowledge, our
contrivances—we who inhabit this planet we call
our own, a planet on loan from the universe.

For the swirl of the galaxies and the quiet
music of the heavens, for the glorious chaos of it all,
for a home among the stars, our thanks.

Sally Zakariya's Pushcart Prize-nominated poetry has appeared in some 70 print and online journals and anthologies and won prizes from Poetry Virginia and the Virginia Writers Club. She is the author, most recently, of *When You Escape* (Five Oaks Press, 2016), as well as *Insectomania* (2013) and *Arithmetic and other verses* (2011), both published by Richer Resources Publishing (RRP).

A former magazine writer and editor, Sally also has experience in publication design and has self-published illustrated alphabet books on anatomy, food, books, and other topics. She designed and produced *Joys of the Table* (RRP, 2015), an anthology of poems about food and eating that she conceived and edited.

With the support of RRP, for whom she serves as occasional poetry editor, Sally blogs at www.butdoesitrhyme.com.

She lives with her husband, an Islamic calligrapher, and their two cats in Arlington, Virginia.

www.ingramcontent.com/pod-product-compliance
Lightning Source LLC
LaVergne TN
LVHW041519070426
835507LV00012B/1695